BE STILL

Spiritual Self-Care for
Mental Health Professionals

Dr. LaRonda Starling

Grace Psychological
HEALTH SERVICES, PLLC

Proofread and Formatted by Polgarus Studio
Edited by Christian Editing Services
Cover by Rob Williams - Designer
(Fiverr.com/cal5086)

Printed in the United States of America

ISBN-13: 978-0-9980462-1-1 (paperback)
ISBN-13: 978-0-9980462-7-3 (ebook)

Dedication

To my loving Father God, thank You for Your love, for Jesus my Savior, and for my life. Thank You for the book idea and the words that You gave me to write. God, I do not have enough words to express my deep gratitude to You for who You are and how You continuously change my life. I am nothing and have never been anything apart from You. You are my rock!

A Beginning Note

Hello and welcome to the book. I hope you enjoy your reading time as much as I enjoyed the time I spent writing. Except where noted and cited, the words and the ideas expressed and written in this book are mine, and no story anyone else has ever shared with me was written or inspired what is written in this book. These are my words, thoughts, and examples, and they were not inspired by anyone I have ever met or not met, including but not limited to family, friends, colleagues, previous coworkers, past and present employers, associates, acquaintances, store clerks, strangers, clients, students, or people on and off the internet. Well, let's just say everybody except the God of the heavens and the Earth.

While I did thoroughly enjoy writing every word, I am not offering this book as advice to anyone, and the information here was written because God told me to. Nothing written in this book can replace the guidance and recommendations of one's own personal treatment specialists (i.e., therapist, psychiatrist, primary care physician). It is not my intention by writing and publishing this book to provide here any advice or therapeutic services of any kind, including but not limited to: evaluation, assessment, diagnosis, therapy, consultation or treatment.

Contents

Introduction

Hello Fellow Mental Health Professional,

Welcome to your first moment of being still. Well, technically you are not being still because you are reading, and thus your brain is actively processing, but I pray for you to have a few moments to rest as you read a portion of this book each day.

Please know I have prayed for you. If you are reading this book because your soul is weary from the work that you do, I have prayed that God would refresh your soul and give you strength. If you are new to the field of helping professionals and you are reading this book to learn the importance of self-care while working, then I have prayed for your time in your field to be one of great successes, and for you to have plenty of time to form the habit of being still early in your career. If you are reading this and you do not fall into one of these categories but are interested in the importance of self-care, then my prayer for you is to learn something new to strengthen your relationship with God, and that He refreshes you while you care for people either now or in the future. I pray this in the name of Jesus. Amen.

I sincerely hope you enjoy your reading time.

Take Care and Be Still,
LaRonda

1: The Importance of Being Still

If you walked into your kitchen right now, would the light be on or off? If the light is on and you are not cooking and no one else needs that light, then how long would you plan to leave the light on before turning it off? You may be someone who is sensitive to leaving lights on for long periods of time. Before you go to bed, you turn off all unnecessary lights, and during the day when a room is empty, you either turn off the light yourself or ask someone else to do it, for one of at least two reasons. One, you pay the bills and see lights left on as wasting electricity. Two, if you left them on all the time, the bulbs would go out sooner and need to be replaced. They would literally burn out, and then their usefulness, for which they were originally created, would no longer exist. There would be no more light shining, making it more difficult to do some activities in your home for which you need light.

The difference between people and light bulbs is that you can always go to the store and choose another light bulb from among a variety of lighting choices. You take the light bulb home and replace the old one with the new one, and again you have what you need to successfully navigate through a dark home. The same type of identical light bulb is manufactured many at a time, making them easy to replace. However, there is only one you. As much as some people may seem to be similar, even identical twins are uniquely themselves. Whether you believe it or not, you are you, and God created you for your unique purpose. There is no going to a people store and getting a new you.

Dim Lights

Just as lights can burn out, so can people. The issue of burnout is not a new one; it affects many people across the helping professions. Similar to the financial consequences of leaving your lights on for too long, keeping your own light burning past your limits has a cost. If you have ever been truly burned out, how much were you likely to want to work? Did you even go to work? Some people may not want to go to work, but having no choice, go anyway, thus taking their dim lights to the workplace. When working through burnout (or preventing it before it becomes an issue for you), find out what God thinks about lights and working.

Speaking of light, Jesus says, "In the same way, let your light shine before others, so that they may see your good works and give glory to your Father who is in heaven" (Matthew 5:16 - ESV). Think about your work in the helping profession. How many good works do you perform per day, whether or not you fully recognize them as such while you are doing them? In this verse we learn that by allowing our light to be seen, others will see our good works, and give the honor to God our Father. You will notice Jesus specifically says, "Let your light shine." If you just have the light bulb but no actual light, then your light is no longer shining. If you have ever been a witness to a light slowly fading, you will notice that it will not shine as brightly, and it may even flicker, but it is no longer completely and consistently operating at its full capacity. If you have the ability to help people, but you have become exhausted to the point of no longer going to work or wanting to go to work, have you also stopped letting your light shine?

If you think about it, many reasons could make your light dim in a professional setting: working long hours, working with difficult populations, working in an environment with high emotional conflict, or being continuously overloaded with tasks. Additionally, many daily occurrences of events and circumstances beyond your control may be dimming your light. Every day we are getting closer to the end of time as we understand it to be here on Earth. In Matthew 24, the disciples ask Jesus about the signs of His future arrival. He lists many of them, such as wars, famines, earthquakes, and false prophets. He explains, "Because lawlessness will multiply, the love of many will grow cold" (Matthew 24:12). As we near Christ's return every day, look around our society or glance at social media and see this increase in wickedness and coldness. As this happens, your work as a mental health professional becomes all the more important. As you are needed more, the possibility of burnout or working with a dimmer light increases.

As mental health professionals, we see this wickedness, this lack of loving emotions and behavior, in many forms through what we hear and observe every day. We know firsthand how the love of most people is growing cold in this increasingly sinful world. As people interact with intensifying wickedness, they raise the risks of trauma and hurtful behavior toward others (such as abuse, neglect, dishonesty, or direct and indirect hurtful behavior), thus prompting many of them to seek counseling services for themselves or their family. At this point, as a trained listener/human information processor, you could be in a place of being continually aware of people treating each other in not so loving ways. How cognizant are you of the negative effects of continual exposure to such information? It is entirely possible for our souls to grow weary under a constant barrage of such information.

You may also experience this behavior through your employer or co-workers. Working in a toxic environment would not only drain you emotionally, but could also restrict you spiritually as your soul grows weary of being the light in a dark place. Have you ever worked in a dark place? Perhaps in one with high emotional conflict, as mentioned earlier? If you have not, consider yourself blessed. If you have, God urges you to do the following: "If possible, as far as it depends on you, live at peace with everyone" (Romans 12:18). One could argue it is easy to be at peace with people who want to be at peace with you and increasingly difficult to be at peace with those who do not share your desire for a harmonious situation or relationship. What is important to remember is that whether or not someone wants to be at peace with you, God wants you to live in peace with them, so you have a responsibility to try. Check the verse again and you will see the personal responsibility there—"as far as it depends on you." If you have had a recent conflict with one of your co-workers, then you may want to think about this before going into the next staff meeting. Imagine how different a work environment would be if everyone worked toward peace.

Many problems can lead to potential burnout, and although I have provided some, you can probably think of many others. The reasons, each by themselves or in combination, can lead to a feeling of exhaustion that may be difficult to reverse by certain means (i.e., taking a good nap). Once you reach that level of exhaustion, how likely are you to start contemplating whether you have chosen the correct profession? If your issue is situational to a certain place of employment, you may choose to continue to work there until you are able to find somewhere else to be employed in that career field. However, burnout inspires some people to start researching alternatives, new avenues they may enjoy working that would not be as emotionally draining at the end of the day as their current chosen career.

If you believe God handpicked the mental health profession especially for you, then before you give up on it, consider the great life improvements made by your last client who achieved some or all of their therapeutic goals. Could they have received mental health intervention services from someone else? Sure, but God gave them to you. What if you were the key difference in their progress? I am by no means encouraging you to stay in the profession of helping others if you feel this is not your calling. But before you give up, think through your decision with prayer and the godly, wise counsel of others who know you well and hold your best interests close to their hearts. Find encouragement from a healthy social support network and remind yourself why you chose your profession in the first place.

Some of us may be so far removed from that decision we no longer remember how excited we were to become someone trained to help other people. Do you remember why you decided that you wanted to be a psychiatrist, a psychologist, a counselor, a social worker, a psychiatric nurse, a life coach? Do you remember the day when you were no longer answering the question, "So what are you majoring in?" with "I have no idea"? At some point, you confidently said, "psychology," "counselor education," "social work," or any of the other majors that lead to a helping profession. If you can remember that day, I'm guessing you did not say it with a sad or angry expression on your face, even in your tiredness from studying, anxiety from exams, or frustrations with group project members. You were excited for your future in helping others and perhaps a bit relieved to have finally found a major. Try to remember that feeling when you are tired, angry, or upset and starting to second-guess your choice of career. Remember your light and take good care of it, so you can take good care of others. If you are a professor, the same truth applies to you. Remember your light as you help others learn to shine their lights, so they too can one day take good care of the people they serve.

Weary Souls

In the Bible Paul provides this encouragement: "And let us not grow weary of doing good, for in due season we will reap, if we do not give up" (Galatians 6:9 - ESV). In a world filled with trauma and sin, I understand if you feel avoiding weariness is hard. When Paul tells us not to be weary, he is not at all saying you should not be weary at any point in your life. He simply offers encouragement and provides a prize to look forward to, letting you know your efforts in well-doing will not be in vain. We honor God and bring Him glory in our attempts to help others—to counsel them, to assist them in finding answers to their symptoms and root problems. You may get weary, but it looks as though we are called to come out of that weariness when we recognize it, especially when we find ourselves living in Weariness City, where the population is not just one (believe it or not). If you find yourself vacationing in Weariness City longer than expected, then you may need to learn to take better care of yourself—physically and emotionally, yes, but also spiritually.

Be sure to nourish your soul. As a helping professional, just taking care of your body is not enough. You can follow all of your doctor's orders, eating right and exercising, but if you do not care for your soul, you may begin to have questions about your fatigue that good physical health cannot answer. Many activities are considered self-care for our physical and emotional needs, such as taking a vacation or talking to a friend. These may be relaxing and, yes, very good ways to stop and take care of yourself, but they do not address what we often handle in our world: the spiritual realm.

When you still feel tired no matter how many self-care activities you check off a list, where can you turn to refresh your soul? The attacks on your energy will not always be from the physical realm. They may be entirely spiritual and unseen. Spiritual warfare is real, and it is written, "For our struggle is not against flesh and blood, but against the rulers, against the authorities, against the cosmic powers of this darkness, against evil, spiritual forces in the heavens" (Ephesians 6:12). In verse 11, we are advised to "put on the full armor of God so that you can stand against the schemes of the devil," reminding us that we are fighting in the spiritual realm and not just the physical one. Why would the devil want you to help people live life as a better version of themselves? He doesn't, and if you are so drained that you cannot help them, then he may see an opportunity in your struggle. Think about it for a second. When you are worn out, burned out, and dealing with the trauma of other people's life stories, can you be your best—what God has called you to be for your clients? Self-care is not only important for your own spiritual battles. It is also important for you to take good care of yourself for your clients who are caught in their own spiritual conflicts.

When we chose the helping profession, we chose to walk alongside people who are burdened, and some mental health professionals unintentionally carry those burdens. The Word of God encourages us, saying, "Humble yourselves, therefore, under the mighty hand of God, so that he may exalt you at the proper time, casting all your cares on him, because he cares about you" (1 Peter 5:6–7). God cares for us and the individuals He has given us to help, and here we are reminded it is not necessary to hold on to our worries and cares (not our own and certainly not those belonging to others). We can give them to the only one who can do anything about them—God. We will get weary, but our God does not.

Helping professionals are still humans with some of the same life stressors as the clients we serve, such as relationship struggles and grief; we are not immune from psychiatric suffering. We may know the appropriate coping skills to use in certain situations or with the symptoms we perceive, but this does not keep those symptoms from occurring. We may know the proper tools and interventions for dealing with these issues, but this knowledge will not prevent us from experiencing one or more of them at some point. Should this occur while your soul is weary, the emotional burden you carry may be heavier than you can handle.

We know the importance of taking care of ourselves so that we can take care of others, and we do not want to hold this information at arm's length. We want to practice self-care ourselves. "Come to me, all who labor and are heavy laden, and I will give you rest. Take my yoke upon you, and learn from me, for I am gentle and lowly in heart, and you will find rest for your souls," Jesus says in Matthew 11:28–29 (ESV). In your weariness, are you willing to learn from Jesus so you can experience this rest? Through the studying of God's Word, we can learn many things from Jesus about serving others and having your own time with the Father.

Learning to Be Still

Being still can be unexpectedly tough. If you have the time, you can sit and not move your body, but then you will need to quiet your mind. You will need to stop worrying about the day, about yesterday or tomorrow or months from now. To be successful in most things in life, you will want to plan and think about what you want to do ahead of time. For this reason, many people, especially those who would call themselves planners, think often about what will happen at some future date. But thinking ahead frequently every day can make it difficult to quiet your mind and easier to worry. Remember, Jesus says, "Therefore don't worry about tomorrow, because tomorrow will worry about itself. Each day has enough trouble of its own" (Matthew 6:34). If you do not allow yourself to be in the present because you are worried about tomorrow, which promises to come with a whole new set of troubles, then when will you ever make the time to let your mind just be still?

When your mind is occupied with constant worry even in your still moments, this is likely to lead to fatigue. Though most people who know what you do for a living assume that listening to other people's thoughts and emotions all day is easy, once you have had your first day of mental health intervention work, you know how hard it can be. You know active listening is just that—active. You are not just sitting in a chair, asking, "How does that make you feel?" all day. You are working, cognitively and emotionally, potentially draining you at the end of the day. On a good day when you do not leave work feeling absolutely exhausted, you can return the next day refreshed. On other days, your soul becomes weary, fatigue starts to set in, and you may not have the energy to help your clients—and not just your clients, but your family, friends, and loved ones too.

So here we go. Having discussed the importance of taking care of yourself, let's discuss many ways in which you could rest your weary soul. I am sure my list of self-care for the soul is not exhaustive, but I hope you find a good starting point through reading this book. Some of you may have been serving in your appointed field for a while. Thank you for all that you have done to help those in need. Others of you may not have gotten started yet and would like to know some ways you can care for yourself ahead of time. Either way, I pray God gives you a constant dose of soul refreshment every time you ask Him.

My first instinct was to create a devotional with daily and weekly activities for you to do, but you may be just too busy or tired to add another activity to your schedule. If you are reading anything not related to a client's case, a continuing education course, or one of your own courses (whether as a student or professor), then I would like for this book to be something that does not drain any more of your energy (well, except for the energy you need to read).

If you want practical application, I have added questions to ponder after each chapter. You will notice I did not leave you much space for writing out long, meaningful answers. I hope to give you a guilt-free opportunity to skip any question. If you are interested in the application questions, it may be a good idea to write your answers out in something more personal to you, like a journal. By doing so and dating your answers, you will be able to look back at a later date to see how you have changed.

If you are a forever student like me, when you see questions you have to answer them, and when you finish this book without having done so, you will feel as if you did not complete something. This is when you have to give yourself permission, especially if you are weary and cannot honestly do anything more than read, to do just that. Just read. No one is grading the answers to your questions, and no one will know how many you have completed or if you did not do them at all (unless, of course, you tell them). Enjoy your reading. Take a break from reading when you feel like it, and most importantly, rest in God's love.

Questions

1. On a scale of 1–10, how tired are you at the end of the workday?

2. When you think about spiritual self-care, what are some activities you think of doing?

3. When was the last time you thought about practicing self-care for your soul?

2: Be Still and Know

After you put your clothes in the washing machine, added the detergent, and started the machine, would you stand there peeking into the machine every five minutes to ensure your clothes were being washed? No. If it is a day for doing all of your household chores at once, you will start the washing machine and then go do something else. You trust that when you hear your washing machine has stopped, you will have clean clothes. Why? Well, one answer may be because you know how washing machines work. Another answer may be your washing machine has consistently washed your clothes without your direct supervision every time—unless it breaks, which happened to me one time. My reassurance of what the washing machine was capable of returned as the repairman left.

God is not a washing machine, but He is reliable. Just as we can be sure the washing machine will wash our clothes because that is what it does, we can also know God will take care of our dirty messes, because that is what God does. We can be sure He will do so consistently.

One of my favorite verses reminds us to "be still and know." The whole verse is "Be still, and know that I am

God. I will be exalted among the nations, I will be exalted in the earth!" (Psalm 46:10 - ESV). Sometimes, unexpected events happen. You are writing case notes when you get an emergency call from one of your clients. Or after a busy day of work, you are home, ready to relax, when you get a call that something unexpected has happened to one of your loved ones. Life can be stressful and busy. So what are we called to do in the busyness of it all? Take some time to be still. Not only to be still, but to know that God is God. What do we know about God that we can reflect on in a difficult or busy time?

This chapter will not provide an exhaustive list of all of the characteristics of God. As a matter of fact, one of the characteristics of God is that He is incomprehensible to our human understanding, meaning even if we knew everything we could about Him, we would still not understand some things. Given what we do know, I think it is fair to say that whatever we do not know is good. The more we learn what God has revealed about Himself, the more we are able to understand His plans for the world and ourselves.

The characteristics of God we will discuss in this chapter are sovereignty, omnipresence, omniscience, and consistency, because as I think about the work of a mental health professional, I have highlighted these characteristics in my mind. If you did some research on the many traits of God in light of your own situation, you may find other characteristics to be comforting to you. The main question to think about when you do your research: How does knowing this about God help me trust Him more, so I can rest in Him and not lean on my own understanding or strength? If you lean on your own understanding all of the time, at some point you will get it wrong, since we are not perfect people. Likewise, if you lean on your own strength, you will eventually feel the pangs of burnout, because the strength you need to get through the weariness in your soul can only come from the Lord.

Sovereign

God is sovereign. He is powerful and has authority over the heavens and the earth, which He created including the people in it—our family, our friends, ourselves, the people we serve, and the people whom we encounter while serving those people. God is also sovereign over all of our circumstances and all of our clients' circumstances. God ordained you to be the mental health practitioner for any particular client before that person called your office for help, and even before that person began to encounter whatever difficulty led them to pick up the phone to call.

When we falsely believe we are the ones in charge and have the ultimate authority over our lives, then we walk on a slippery slope that can lead to disappointment when people do not behave the way we think they should, or when circumstances do not occur in the manner we hoped. Once you learn God is in control, you see the world from a different perspective. You begin to see circumstances in a different way and your expectations will change. For example, you may be feeling the symptoms of burnout because you feel you are not making much of a difference in the lives of some of your clients. If you believe their success in therapy solely depends on your skills and knowledge, then you may begin to take the failures that naturally occur too personally. If you remember God is in control, and maybe the person is not meant to experience great improvements with you, but maybe God has sent them to you so they will have someone to listen to them even without an intention of changing behavior, then your perspective of the situation will be different. If God's assignment for you in the life of this person is just to listen to them, then when you have done so, you will be successful in God's eyes.

If you have been in your field for any length of time, then think of a time when something at work did not go the way you expected it to. How did you respond in that situation? If I had to guess, you responded based on the way you processed the situation. If you did not consider the sovereignty of God, then you may have missed an important angle in handling your disappointment, your hurt, and your frustration. Thinking about the sovereignty of God encourages us to consider the grand scheme of things, how the situation relates to God's plan for the lives of the people involved. God has a plan. He always has a plan, and He is in charge.

Omnipresent

Our Father is also omnipresent. He is everywhere at all times. Because of this, anytime you feel overwhelmed because you cannot be everywhere you want to be at one time, you can be confident in knowing God is everywhere you are unable to go. When your clients leave your office after having decided to make a major change in their lives, you cannot follow them around for the next six days to ensure this happens. Worrying about them is not going to increase the likelihood of them completing that life change, nor will it give you any extra time back. Remember how Jesus feels about worry in Matthew 6:34. He says not to worry about tomorrow because there will be plenty to worry about when that day arrives. If you should not worry about what happens the next day in your life, then you should not worry about what is happening in other people's lives. Now, I am not in any way saying you should not care. Of course, you should care and plan for the next session. However, caring and planning can be done without worrying.

As you attempt to quiet your mind, remember God is everywhere. He sees your clients trying to change when you cannot. Even for those who are not ready to change, He sees that too. He walks with them daily, just as He walks with you. Try having faith in God's omnipresence enough to understand that when you cannot see the people you help, God can see them. He cares about them too, and in His own way.

So, yes, one part of you being still is the knowledge God is everywhere, watching over your clients and the communities you serve. Similarly, He is watching over you and walking with you through the many joys and discouragements of being a helping professional. Think about the person you are most close to now, maybe a family member, a friend, a mentor, or someone else. Why are you close to that person? There is a chance that one of the reasons for the closeness of that relationship is the time you spend or have spent with that individual. Well, whether you know it or not, the amount of time you spend with that person, even if it is every day of your life, pales in comparison to the time you spend with God. Jeremiah shares that the Lord told him, "Before I formed you in the womb I knew you, and before you were born I consecrated you; I appointed you a prophet to the nations" (Jeremiah 1:5 - ESV). So, what is God telling Jeremiah? He tells him that before he was even conceived by his parents, God knew him. Reading this, it is fair to say God is the first person who knew you, so He has known you the longest. Because He is omnipresent, you have never been out of His sight from the moment He first knew you. God lovingly walks with you everywhere, whether you are working at the full force of your skill set or actively being still.

Omniscient

Think of the satisfying feeling that comes from not knowing something at first and then finally figuring out the answer. You get a lyric stuck in your head, sing it to yourself all day, and accidentally let it slip out. Someone hears you and asks for the name of the song. You have no idea, so you keep singing it, hoping it will spark name recognition. Before the days of the smartphone, you would have had to wait for the song to come on the radio and for the DJ to announce its name. You could also have gone around singing the song to your family and friends, waiting for them to remember the name of the song. These days, with only a few portions of the lyrics typed in an internet search engine, you can find the name quickly.

Life is different. It is not as easy to figure things out. You can type a question about life into an internet search engine and find all manner of answers without having confidence that any of them are correct. You can ask friends, family, and anyone else you encounter in your walk of life, and you will learn different perspectives. But some things only God knows. "Trust in the LORD with all your heart, and do not rely on your own understanding" (Proverbs 3:5). Notice there are two directives here, and doing one allows you to be able to do the other. The verse states we should not lean or heavily rely on our own understanding. This is in no way saying you should not understand something as much as you can. Some things in life you will not understand, and so it is quite easy not to lean on your comprehension of events. However, when you do have a good understanding of what is happening, it may be hard not to rely on that understanding. In other words, when we understand something and can make sense of it from our point of view, it may be difficult not to hold tight to that understanding or make a decision based solely on our own knowledge before praying. So, the first part of the verse is very important—we are to trust God. Trust God when you do not understand, and especially trust Him when you have a partial or possibly full understanding. One reason we can trust the Lord is that we know He knows everything. God knows why you are feeling tired. He knows all of your circumstances, and He knows what it is going to take to bring your soul peace.

God is all-knowing or omniscient. When you do not have the answers, God does. When you are trying to figure out a client's difficulties or make a new career move, God already knows how it will work out and what you should do next. Because of this, it is advisable to ask Him and follow His guidance instead of only relying on your own understanding of these situations. If you are a mental health practitioner, then you went to school for a long period of time, learning all that you could about how the brain works, about people's behaviors and emotional reactions, and how to intervene when the latter becomes an issue. As a student you learned to do research and find answers. The answers to those questions were easily a library book away, a search query away via an internet library, or in one of the many textbooks you did not sell back to the bookstore. There will come a time in your life when you will not know the answer, and no matter how much you research, no matter how much you seek out an answer from other people, you will not reach a satisfactory conclusion. In those times as in every time, God knows. Trust Him.

Consistent

Let's say you go to a restaurant on a Monday and have a good experience with the food and customer service. You enjoy it so much you decide to take a friend back there on

Friday, but you may not have the same experience if the cook is not feeling well and overcooking all the food and if your waitstaff is not in a good mood, providing you with mediocre customer service. This inconsistency in your experiences may play a role in your future decisions to eat at that restaurant again. Some people are similar to this restaurant. They may present as one way or treat you one way on certain days in certain situations, but on other days they may present in a completely different manner. When you are presented with this change in person or behavior, it may leave you confused about who they really are.

In a world where we have to deal with people who may be one way today and completely different tomorrow, I thank God He is consistent. He is who He is all the time. "Jesus Christ is the same yesterday, today, and forever" (Hebrews 13:8). When someone is consistently who they are, you know you can depend on them; they are trustworthy and can be relied on during any situation. That is how God is in our lives. He is consistently sovereign, consistently omnipresent, consistently omniscient, and consistent in every other trait He possesses. In your work as a mental health practitioner you can be assured God cares about every situation you encounter on a daily basis, because He always has, and He does not change.

The most amazing aspect of God's consistency is that He is the same God no matter how much we change our feelings or our dependency on Him. Some people only pray when they are in the midst of circumstances beyond their control. In doing so, they are only acknowledging God's sovereignty in times when they feel desperate. What they are also relying on in those times is God's omnipresence, His capability of being right where they are whether or not it has been a while since they've called on Him. The important thing to remember is that God is always sovereign and omnipresent, whether or not we are acknowledging Him as such.

When we understand God is consistent, we can be still in His unchanging power. God can be seen as consistent to those who love Him and are called by Him. Specifically, it is written, "We know that all things work together for the good of those who love God, who are called according to his purpose" (Romans 8:28). Look at the words "all things." This means no matter what happens in life, God is consistently creating good out of everything, even the bad. If you understand that God will create good out of any life circumstance, then you do not have to ruminate about any of those unfortunate and trying situations. Let them go and know that God will use them. Instead, you can be still and wait for God to make something good out of it. You may not know what the good is until we all get to heaven and see God's plan completely unfolded, but for all the ups and downs in life, God can use them all consistently for His purposes.

Knowing God

As I wrote earlier, these characteristics are far from an exhaustive list of the amazing attributes of God. They are good points to remember about God in our daily grind of helping others. If you remember God is sovereign, you will not try to take sole responsibility for the behavior of your clients, co-workers, supervisors, or employees. You will remember that God is in control of all situations inside and outside of the counseling center, private practice, psychiatric hospital, church, school, or wherever you work. If you remember God is omnipresent, you will know you do not have to wait until you get to church to pray about something, because you can talk to Him right where you are at any time. If you remember God is omniscient, you can rest in knowing that what you do not know, God knows. The client issue you cannot figure out? God already understands. When you remember God is consistent, whenever He moves you from one job assignment to the next, you can rest assured He will provide what is needed to make a smooth transition every time.

So how does knowing more about God help you to be still? Good question. If you have worked somewhere where your salary or hourly wage depended on grant money, then at some point you may have wondered what would happen if the grant was not renewed. You could worry every day that you would have to find another job, which you may not enjoy as much, or work for free in your current position— or you could be still. You could refuse to worry and quiet your mind, trusting God is your provider. You could tell yourself, "I can be still and not worry about my finances, because God is a provider."

Sometimes life can get lonely. At times, you may feel physically lonely because no one is around. Other times you may feel alone emotionally because you believe no one understands how you feel or the current circumstance that has led you to become weary. Not understanding that God is everywhere can leave you in this lonely state, because in your mind no one is with you. In these times, you may try to escape the discomfort of loneliness by doing what many people do to avoid this feeling: choosing unhealthy ways to cope such as substance use or toxic relationships. In these times, however, if you recall God's omnipresence, then you can remember God is everywhere even when you are not focused on that fact. You are, in fact, not alone, no matter what lies you have been led to believe. God is there for you to talk to. He understands you in a way even the best of your friends cannot. You can be still in a lonely time, and because God is omnipresent, you are never really alone.

Questions

1. What are some of the other names of God (e.g., Jehovah Shalom—"The Lord is Peace") and what do they mean?

2. Of all of the characteristics of God, which one means the most to you right now? Why?

3. Complete the following sentence: I can be still about _____ (add a circumstance you are struggling with right now) because God is _____ (add a characteristic of God here).

3: Be Still and Pray

Imagine a few friends who have decided to go to a restaurant for dinner. They are greeted and seated by the hostess and given menus. Everything on the menu looks delicious: appetizers, salads, sandwiches, chicken and steak entrees, plenty of fish and shrimp options for the seafood lovers, and three pages of desserts. Imagine this restaurant has the kitchen, chef, and staff that can bring the friends anything their hearts desire. All they need to do is order. When the waiter or waitress comes to take the friends' orders, would it be a good idea for them to politely refuse, proceed to the kitchen themselves, and attempt to cook and serve their own meals? Of course not. They should sit at their table, place their orders, and let the restaurant operate as it has been designed in order to provide them with a great dining experience. They can have whatever they want; they just need to ask.

Now, I am not comparing heaven to this kitchen nor the Lord to a chef. Certainly, we do not order the Lord to do anything, and I feel confident heaven is much better than any kitchen we could imagine—the Father gives us much more than drinks, food, and desserts. However, the principle stands. Why would you not ask God for what you need and want if He is willing and able to supply your needs? Why try to figure it all out and do it all yourself without consulting God first, which He wants us to do? God is ready to provide for you, but He is waiting for you to ask. Jesus told this to His disciples, "Truly I tell you, the one who believes in me will also do the works that I do. And he will do even greater works than these, because I am going to the Father. Whatever you ask in my name, I will do it so that the Father may be glorified in the Son. If you ask me anything in my name, I will do it" (John 14:12-14). Believing in Jesus, we will follow His example and perform works (i.e., serving others). Here we are also reminded to pray in the name of Jesus, pointing out the importance of ending a prayer, before saying "Amen", with "in the name of Jesus" or "in Jesus's name."

If you can ask God for anything and talk to Him about every facet in life, then why would you waste time running around frantically, trying to do it all yourself? You would be like those people serving themselves in the restaurant. God has made himself available to His creation, and many times we do not wish to access His power and great gifts until our situation has gotten unbearably unpleasant, but God is there for us to talk to all of the time every day.

As it relates to your exhausted soul, how many times have you felt tired or burned out from work and instead of stopping to ask God for the strength to make it through the day, you tried to rely on your own depleted supply? If God called you to help others, then He is more than capable of supplying what you need to make it through a rough day, week, or season of life. If your direct clinical work is not what has caused your weariness, but you suspect your other life difficulties may be impacting your clinical work, God invites you to tell Him about your experiences, your feelings, your thoughts, and your needs.

Just as we can go to God in prayer during the rough seasons of life, we can also talk to God about the exciting and joyful times in our days. If you are reading this and you are not feeling burned out or experiencing any emotional distress, this does not make your prayers any less important to God. God is available at any time and for any reason that you need to speak with Him. Your part of the communication is to just start talking to Him wherever you are, physically and emotionally and in any life season.

Jesus and Prayer

When thinking about self-care for individuals who dedicate their lives to helping others, there is no better example than Jesus. If you read the Gospel accounts of Jesus's life (Matthew, Mark, Luke, John), you will discover He does many things in His thirty-three years on Earth. Some of His many activities include preaching about the upcoming Kingdom and His second coming, teaching people in a way they would understand, healing the sick, and feeding a multitude of people. Luke writes, "But the news about him spread even more, and large crowds would come together to hear him and to be healed of their sicknesses. Yet he often withdrew to deserted places and prayed" (5:15–16). Look what Luke notes at the end here. Jesus often leaves His ministry to pray.

Another example is given by Mark in his Gospel account:

> When evening came, after the sun had set, they brought to him all those who were sick and demon-possessed. The whole town was assembled at the door, and he healed many who were sick with various diseases and drove out many demons. And he would not permit the demons to speak, because they knew him. Very early in the morning, while it was still dark, he got up, went out, and made his way to a deserted place; and there he was praying. (1:32–35)

Here we see Jesus does it again. He goes somewhere by Himself to pray. Since Luke mentions Jesus went away to pray "often," He likely did that routinely. While we do not have the "whole city" gathering at our office doors for help all at once, we may have some days that certainly feel this way. Jesus shows us here an optimal way to refresh by taking some time to get away and talk to the Father.

Luke and Mark are not the only ones who documented this behavior demonstrated by Jesus. Matthew writes, "After dismissing the crowds, he went up on the mountain by himself to pray. Well into the night, he was there alone" (14:23). If you read around this verse, you will notice right before this Jesus feeds the five thousand people, and after this He walks on water. At the end of the chapter, He arrives at another place to heal the sick. Between these important events something significant is shown: Jesus takes time to break away from people to pray.

Jesus does two things in the examples noted here that I believe would aid the spiritual self-care of a helping professional: 1) He prays; 2) He goes to meet the Father in a place where He could pray uninterrupted. In the busyness of our plugged-in society and in a profession where we are likely in constant contact with people, it is a sweet time to sit alone with God, talking to Him about your thoughts and feelings.

Think about your workday or even your workweek and how many of other people's thoughts and feelings you process even if they are not your clients. Have you ever gotten yourself in a conversation at the grocery store or somewhere else with someone you do not know? It is likely because of your listening skills; you made them feel heard. Unlike many others in society, you have a unique skillset in that you have been taught the most effective way to listen. Who listens to you when you really feel that you need to be heard? Some mental health practitioners may have other people in their social support networks who are good listeners, while others take their life concerns to their own therapists. Remember that whether or not you are in therapy or have a good sounding board in another non-practitioner person, God is always there to listen. Yes, you can go to therapy and also pray about what is going on in your life. It does not have to be an either/or situation. Praying alone to God in a time where your attention is undivided can refresh the soul and be a good way to build a relationship with the Father.

Alone with God

Have you ever been somewhere with someone who has a difficult time detaching from their phone or other electronic device and being present with you in the moment? It may seem as though their electronic device is an add-on to their hands. If your work requires you to be on call, then this behavior is understandable. For everyone else, it is possible to go for some length of time without the constant use of an electronic device that connects you at every hour of the day with other people. If you want to spend a few quiet moments alone to be refreshed, so you are not taking phone calls at that time, but you are online where people gather for social interaction in some other manner, then you are still engaged in some way with others and not completely alone.

Some people do not like to be alone for various reasons. Some of them have not yet learned of the omnipresence of God. Understanding this, you know you are never alone. You are sometimes without the presence of another earthly human being, but you are never truly alone. Even right now, if you are reading this book in a place where your family and friends are not, your number-one Family Member and Friend is here with you. Stop reading for a second and say hello to God. He can hear you and wants to hear from you.

Another issue that people often have with being still and praying is the actual praying part. There are those who feel they do not know how to pray. When the disciples asked Jesus how to pray, He gave them a model prayer (Matthew 6:9–13). There are many important takeaways from this prayer. One of the relevant lessons for our self-care discussion is to just talk to God. You are not going to say anything that could surprise Him. He knows your heart. So, if you are afraid that you are not going to have the perfect words or that your prayers do not contain as many eloquent words as another person's, pray anyway. The Father wants to hear from you, what you are thinking, how you are feeling, and how you are experiencing this life.

Some of my most heartfelt prayers have been me just talking to God in the moment—at home, in the office, in the car, or in the store—praying for patience because I am waiting in a long line. Does God care that I need an extra dose of patience in the store? Absolutely. Does He care if I ask perfectly in some long, eloquent monologue for everyone to hear, using the perfect words? Absolutely not. As a matter of fact, Jesus gives the directive to pray in a "private room" (Matthew 6:6). He also reminds us God the Father already knows what we want, so just ask Him. Because we can go to Him with our needs, Jesus warns us against using "many words" with no meaning (Matthew 6:7).

The Model Prayer

If you have gotten to this point and you continue to be unsure of what to say in your prayers, we can once again turn to Jesus for His example. The entire prayer can be found in Matthew 6:9–13. If you study it line by line and take the time to understand what Jesus reveals about prayer, it is amazing. His prayer begins and ends with who the Father is, where He is, and His unending power. Between these praises and acknowledgements are some very important situations to pray for.

First, Jesus asks the Father for "daily bread." He may be just asking the Father to provide Him with whatever food He needs for that day. I am grateful we can pray for our food. Food is good. But think about what else you need in daily doses in order to continue to be encouraged. Do you need patience? Do you need to be a little more kindhearted today than you were yesterday? Do you need to speak more gently when talking to your employer, employees, and/or co-workers? Some of us might work in a situation where we only need to ask for patience on Monday to be carried through to Friday or Saturday; some of us may need to ask the Lord for daily doses of patience.

The next thing Jesus prays for is forgiveness. Now, Jesus is sinless, so remember He is teaching His disciples how to pray, and they, like us, are sinners. Yes, if you are reading this, you are a sinner. You may have not sinned in the last five minutes, but wait for it. Because we do sin, we are in special need of this next part of the verse asking God to forgive us as we forgive others. People will lie, steal, and commit adultery and other sins against other people. When you are one of the people who has committed the action against another, you can ask God to forgive you. Also, when you are the victim of sin, then you are to forgive the people who sinned against you. The Lord feels it is important to forgive others, and if you have a hard time forgiving someone who has wronged you, especially if they are unapologetic, then you could start asking for daily doses of the strength to forgive.

After mentioning forgiveness, Jesus asks to be able to be delivered or freed from the enemy and not fall into the trap of temptation. See, sin is often very tempting. Asking God to help us in this way is increasingly important as we live in a world where we are promised a multiplication of "lawlessness," not a proliferation of goodness (Matthew 24:12). With increased wickedness, the temptation to do things we know we should not do will grow, and asking God to help us in this way benefits the soul. What is tempting you to sin right now? In what ways do you need to be delivered from the enemy?

Before we move to the next section, I think it is important to mention that there are always other ways we can pray, other things we can pray for, and other ways we can pray for other people. If we take some time to study the Bible and read about the first Christians, who were there for each other, one of the things we learn is that they prayed for each other for various reasons. In times of weariness and burnout, it may be beneficial for you to ask someone to pray for you and for you to pray for others.

Your Time with God

How many times have you had something exciting happen in your day and could not wait to call someone to tell them what happened? Or if you are a social media aficionado, how quick are you to post these exciting things online for your family, friends, and a few million strangers to read? What about things that make you sad? What about the things that make you weary? How different would your life be if you put the phone down and moved away from your computer or tablet and found a quiet place to talk to the Father? God wants that time from you to talk to Him and express your need for Him over all others and all other things.

Luke says Jesus went out to the wilderness, and Mark notes Jesus went to a "deserted" place. Where is your place to be alone? If you live alone, finding a quiet place may be easier than it would be if you lived in a home with other people. However, living alone does not mean you will be free from electronic distraction. You want to get away from your phone and computer. If you live in a household with other people, where can you find a place to talk to God by yourself? You may find it difficult if your household is full and busy, but be creative. Is there anywhere you can go in your house where someone will not follow you? If you have a small child who is competing with your shadow, that answer may be no. When they first go to sleep or just before they wake up, can that be your time?

Sometimes when you are in the middle of battling the struggles of this life (financial difficulties, time management, family illnesses), you become so overwhelmed you do not know what to pray. Allow gratefulness to set in, knowing we are loved by a God who made plans for such a scenario. "In the same way the Spirit also helps us in our weakness, because we do not know what to pray for as we should, but the Spirit himself intercedes for us with unspoken groanings" (Romans 8:26). A study of this passage will reveal that when we do not know what to pray, the Holy Spirit living inside of us will intercede for us to the Father. Prayer is conversation with God. In the same way you would tell a friend about what is going on in your life, you can tell God about your worries, hopes, and desires.

When you are ready to begin to have an alone time with God, resist the pressure you may feel to have your quiet time at the same time as other people's. If you look at the two written accounts of Jesus slipping away to pray, you will see one verse says He went "early morning, while it was still dark," and the other that He went "often" without specifying a time. Only you know what is the best time for you to actually sit and be physically and mentally still.

In taking some time out of each day for a regular quiet time, you can rest, even if it is only for a small amount of time, and begin to get closer to God as you bring your thankfulness and concerns to lay at His feet. If you have ever had a good friend, someone who is consistently there for you almost every time you call, you may recall how it feels to be heard, to know this person is listening to you, especially when you are spending most of your time being the listener in your profession. Imagine how much better you will feel when you talk to your True Friend, someone who loves and cares for you and knows your situation intimately and can do something about it. I am in no way discounting the love and support of a good friend, because I know that sometimes those friends can be sent by God Himself. But just as you spend time talking with friends and being vulnerable with them, building stronger relationships with them, you can spend time and be vulnerable with God.

I should let you know something very important before we move on to the next chapter. When you start to spend time with God in this way, you may find you can be physically still but mentally restless, recalling events and conversations from the day before and rehearsing what you would like to do the next day. Every possible distraction that you can think of may occur, and some you may not readily recognize as something that is distracting you from praying alone to God or having a still, quiet time with Him. These distractions could be something that is happening around you in your quiet time place (e.g., ringing phone, screaming children) or something that is going on in your mind. You may all of a sudden find the time to make your mental grocery list or a host of other tasks when you try to quiet your mind. Struggling to focus is a possibility, but God is more than capable of assisting you with keeping your mind and your conversation solely with Him.

Questions

1. Do you have somewhere where you can go to be alone with God?

2. What time of the day is the best time for you to be still and alone in the presence of God?

3. If you cannot think of a time in the day, what is keeping you from having that time?

4: Be Still and Reflect

Have you ever looked in a mirror? Depending on what type of mirror you are standing in front of, you will appear different ways. If you stand in front of a fun-house mirror, you may see reflected back at you a distorted version of yourself. You know in reality you do not have those dimensions, but because of what you are looking at, you know you do not look like yourself. When you look into a normal mirror in the morning, you see reflected back the real version of yourself. If you look into a magnifying mirror, you may be able to see every imperfection on your face, even ones you had not known existed.

Depending on your self-esteem and how you are feeling any particular day, you may not care that the fun-house mirror made you look as though your ears were bigger than they actually are, that your reflection in the normal mirror reminded you of the pounds you have gained, or that the close-up mirror pointed out how you are getting a little older year after year. If given the opportunity, most people would prefer to look into a mirror where everything on their body is the size they believe it should be. If it were this type of mirror, then your pants would appear to fit well, even if they felt a little tight from the weight gain. If the close-up mirror were one that most people would prefer, then when you looked at the skin on your face, it would appear smooth and unblemished.

Now, this last type of mirror does not exist, but when we reflect only on our flaws or someone else's distorted view of our imperfections, this will bring up negative emotions. When we can reflect on something positive, such as how good the shirt looks instead of how you wish the pants looked differently, then you can set your mind on what you admire about yourself and avoid dwelling on only what you wish would change. If you have had to teach your clients how to change their maladaptive thoughts to rational, healthy ones, then this information may not be new to you.

Some of our dwelling on only the negative may lead to feelings of weariness and burnout. If you only reflect on the negative moments you have had in the profession or at your current place of employment, then it will be difficult to see even the smallest bit of joy in each day. Think about how differently your day would go if you chose to reflect on things in another way. If you think about how good you look in your shirt, then you may be willing to ignore how tight your pants feel around your waist. If you concentrate on the good in your workday, then while you may not ignore the difficulties in the day, they will definitely not be your focus. Our thoughts are powerful and learning to focus on the good takes hard work, but it is not impossible.

Godly Reflections

In the Bible you will find the following verse: "Finally, brothers, whatever is true, whatever is honorable, whatever is just, whatever is pure, whatever is lovely, whatever is commendable, if there is any excellence, if there is anything worthy of praise, think about these things" (Philippians 4:8 - ESV). How many times have you ended your day reflecting on the day? How much of this reflection focused on the trying times you experienced? I wonder how different the walk from the office to the car would be if on the way we only thought about these just, pure, and lovely things. Depending on your work setting, you may have eight hours or more of thinking on things that are not honorable, pure, or lovely with no meaningful break. How would you say it affects you to think about what you hear on a daily basis after your workday ends? Do you ever feel emotionally and/or mentally exhausted at the end of the day? How do you think this will affect you if this happens too many days, weeks, months, or years in a row?

Although there are many reasons to think about and process the negative aspects of this world, thinking about the positive would be more refreshing. Some days, it may be more difficult to flip the thought switch from negative to positive as soon as you walk out of the office, but in the interest of self-care it may be worth a try. If you are working in a situation where you see clients with only a few minutes between each person, you may find it helpful to take those minutes, if possible, to refresh your mind by reflecting on positive thoughts or events.

Thoughts of Truth

If you take a look back at the Philippians verse, the first thing we are encouraged to think about is something true. A number of emotions and thoughts can rob your ability to be still, including anxiety and defeat. For example, if you are working with a difficult population where actual, consistent life change is a rarity, you may begin to feel defeated. If you add to your discouragement defeated thoughts such as, "It does not matter what I say or teach my client, they will never change," then you have started down a road toward chronic disappointment. In this case, you see that the negative thought is not something you know to be a fact. It is not possible for you to know this person will never change. Even if you are never a witness to the change, it is very possible for this individual to transform. Remember that if God is powerful enough to create all things, He is powerful enough to soften hearts and change people's thoughts about how they should behave. What would happen if we changed this defeated thought of believing that a client or client population will never change to something we know to be true?

This is where we try. If you change the defeated thought to something you know to be true, such as, "No matter what I teach my client, the decision for them to change belongs to them," then you have the potential to change your view of each situation and your work at the agency or your practice. Acknowledging that the responsibility for the change belongs to the client and not you may change your way of thinking about your work. The client who is not making significant changes while in therapy could make progress after they are no longer receiving therapeutic services from you. Your role in their life may have just been to provide the psychoeducation they will use later. Sure, it would be rewarding to get to see every client goal reached, but no matter how hard you try, sometimes they will reach those goals and we may never know. Reminding yourself that you did what you were trained to do (listen, reflect, reframe, etc.), and that is your responsibility; then you may start to see more cases as a win.

Has someone ever lied to you? Have you ever lied to someone? While some people can lie and stick to the lie with an identical story every time, other people lie to you and every time you hear the story something has changed. That is because they could not remember the first story they told you, and so you got a different account, with neither story being all the facts. The thing about facts is they remain the same each time you hear them. The more you hear the fact, the more you will be able to quickly recall it. The first time you learned simple arithmetic problems, you likely had to count farm animals on a worksheet, draw out lines on a sheet of paper, or count on your fingers. After you learned the truth of one and one being two every time, you no longer needed the visual assistance. In this same way, your positive and truthful thoughts may become automatic if you reflect on them often enough in a meaningful manner.

Thoughts of Excellence

Have you ever taught at a college or university, trained a group, or provided a continuing education seminar to colleagues? If you have, then it is likely you have received evaluations. Living in a world where at least one person is openly offended by the smallest nonissue and some find complaining a source of entertainment, you are certain to get that one review, even if you know you did a great job. That one review says you are horrible, and you should never teach, train, or present anything ever again in life. If you receive that one review and all the other reviews are positive, which one are you more likely to think about when you are done? Sometimes the not-so-good reviews provide you with constructive criticism on what to do better next time, but the good reviews, which are likely to be the majority of your reviews, should not be ignored. Some of your evaluations will likely be written by the encouragers in your class, and they probably point out aspects of your skill in the classroom, so reflect on the good you see and think about what is excellent.

When you are tempted to think only negatively about the work you are doing as a mental health professional, you might forget to contemplate the good aspects of your workday. Even when working with the most difficult of populations, remember that they have chosen to receive services from your place of employment. You may ask, "What if they are mandated by some agency (i.e., the judicial system)?" Well, they still could have not shown up for services and dealt with the consequences. I am not sure how often that may happen, but because there are people in jail and prison, one could hypothesize that at least a few of them failed to follow judge's orders and were made to face the full consequences of their actions. So, when someone is mandated to receive services from your office or agency and their level of motivation to change their behavior is low (which may not be all cases), their arriving to your office may be all they are capable of in that moment. They made it to their appointment, which in that moment can be excellent. When an excellent thought is not one of a grand victory, reflect on a small, excellent win instead. They are there. Sometimes you just have to look harder to find them.

When you have reached a place in your career where you feel you are not having success often enough, do not forget to reflect on all the times when you were able to exhibit excellence yourself in some way. Maybe your excellence is not career focused. It is possible for you to be excellent in other areas of life. What are those for you? These can range from how well you perform volunteer duties during your time off, to something as simple as how good you are at that game you play on your phone during your downtime.

Thoughts of Praise

Additionally, we are called to think of things that are worthy of praise. What a great number of things we have every day that are worth praising God for. Even if you have just had one of your least favorite days at work, praiseworthy aspects of that day are there somewhere. They may be more hidden on some days, but they are there. We can praise God for things people usually take for granted, such as waking up every day, having a job, having clothes to wear, and having a breakfast before you get started. You can praise God for events in the day that may not involve you but are praises about other people. The point is to choose a time in the day to reflect on something worthy of praise.

Some people remember to give God praise when His blessings are grand and can easily be seen by ourselves and others. There are others who are really good at praising God for what some would consider the little things. Then there are others who, when they feel that their lives are falling apart, and constant episodes of tearfulness and nagging doubt whisper to them that they will not get better, praise God through their pain. Praising God in any situation reminds us of God's power in our life and can help us to recall those characteristics of God that help us to know more about Him, so we can have faith in His promises and be still in Him.

On the days when it is difficult to recall a positive situation or reflect on the praiseworthiness of God, what could be used to assist your memory? Oftentimes, lists or journals will put those encouraging events in our lives within our reach when we are in deep need of something good to think about. At times you may face a whole burdensome day, week, or year, and as you look back, you just cannot bring yourself to reflect on anything good. Think back to good times in the past, even moments many years ago. In this age of oversharing, you may be tempted to choose to look at someone else's life and think about how God is blessing them. That may be a slippery slope to coveting (wanting something that someone else has), so think about your own experiences with God first, still praising Him for the good work He has done in the lives of others when you truly feel thankful.

Journaling Thoughts

During times of stress and weariness, we can easily get caught up in general negativity and current life struggles, but if you pay close attention, every once in a while, you will see a glimmer of light. Perhaps your workday was bad, but when you went to fuel your car for the rest of the week, the gas station was offering free car washes and smoothies. I know this may not be likely to happen, but such a victory, while small, is a great time to reflect on the fact that something in your day was unexpectedly nice. Those small things make for good journaling to review later, when all you can think about is the unpleasantness and wickedness in the world. Remember God is sovereign, and when these sorts of events happen, they may be God's way of telling you He sees and cares about you.

If your exhaustion is not from negative, untrue thoughts or if you are already operating from a heart of praise on a daily basis, remember the other things in Philippians 4:8 we are called to think about (things that are just, pure, lovely). These things may be personal to you, so consider writing them in your praise list/journal. This way when you are having a tough time coming up with something on your own in a fit of tiredness, these examples are right at your disposal.

Career Reflections

Why did you decide to become a mental health professional? If you are new to the profession or have not gotten started, then the answer to this question may be fresh on your mind. Some common answers may be your desire to help people or that others have said you are a good listener, so you decided to use your natural ability to guide your career choice. A more personal answer may be having a good therapy experience from a time when you were the client. If it has been a while since you started, you may not remember why you decided to make the choice for this career, or perhaps you remember the emotional pull you used to feel to a life of serving others, but now it is not as strong.

Before you give up in a fit of exhaustion, sit and reflect on your decision. If there were good friends or classmates to whom you talked at the time, it may be beneficial to tell them about how you feel now, as the best of them may boost your spirits with a memory of your motivations. We learned from Jesus's time of prayer that some things are better done alone and in secluded places, but not everything. You may need wise counsel, especially when you are having a difficult time remembering why you wanted to help people in the first place. If you are usually the wise counsel among your friends and are lacking in this area when you need it, then it is prayer time. You can ask the Lord to send you wise counsel and the support you need at any time.

Once you remember the reasons you decided to become a therapist, compare them to your reasons for wanting to give up and reflect on them. How many of the reasons are out of your control? How many of them are in your control? If you feel the Father has called you into this profession, have you talked to Him about wanting to leave? Sometimes you will experience the sweet relief of God moving you from one job situation to another, and at other times, you may conclude He has not called you away yet, and instead He is inviting you to remain in your current position until some appointed time.

Wise Counsel

While reflecting on your career and the reasons you are experiencing a fatigue that physical rest is not fixing, then consulting God about your thought habits may help you think through things differently—especially if the reasons for your fatigue are life stressors. Remember, just knowing a bit more than the general population about how to cope with life stressors will not make you immune from them, nor allow you to immediately think of the appropriate coping skill every time you feel stressed. If anyone in the Bible knew about experiencing difficulties, Job certainly did. If you have never heard of his story, Job was a God-fearing man who had a family and many riches. Satan was allowed to test him, and Job lost it all. He lost his children, his livestock, and his employees. And after all of that, he was afflicted with a skin disease. In a response to his friends, he said, "With God are wisdom and might; he has counsel and understanding" (Job 12:13 - ESV). This is a very true statement and an important reason to pray to ask God for understanding about your current level of weariness. Ask Him to counsel you in this difficult time. God's perspective on our lives differs from our own, and I wonder how much change we would see if we would ask God to help us reflect on our lives in the way that He does. Even amid his pain and struggle, Job still remembered that God is wise.

So far, most of the ways we have discussed being still have involved doing things alone with God (e.g., praying, reflecting). However, it is important to remember that we do not live as individuals without the direct or indirect influence of the other people God allows in our lives (i.e., our families, friends, colleagues). For this reason, God may provide wise people who will help lead you in the right direction. They may assist by offering to walk alongside you in a difficult moment of life or by being what many people need, a listening ear.

I have also found that sometimes God may allow certain individuals to be a part of one of your life stories so other individuals (believers and nonbelievers) can see the power of God. Pray you are able to discern that the person or people who come into your life during a rough season will actually be sent by God. Taking bad advice, or what may have initially sounded like good advice from the wrong person, may lead you to a worse place than you were in before you spoke with them. But when you can receive wise counsel from someone who has consistently helped you to navigate through life, then you may find it helpful to spend some time reflecting on life decisions with them.

Finally, many times as a helper, you may have difficulty reaching out to people when you need to, but your people are there for a reason. If they are people who are filled with the love of Jesus, then that is a bonus, and in those times when you seek their assistance, you may see how God can use someone in another person's life. Good conversations with helpful and wise friends could give you enough of what you need to handle the stress. As we have been taught and/or just learned through life, communication is important. If the people in your life do not know how you are feeling or what you need, then it may be difficult or impossible for them to help you.

But thinking as a clinician, you and I both know not even the wisest of your friends can help you through certain situations. Either they have no answers for you this time, or they do not have time to give. If this is what you are currently experiencing or if the issue is prolonged, then it may be time to sit on the other side of the counseling room in someone else's client chair. Reflecting on your experiences and life struggles in those moments may be easier with someone who can be more objective with your situation than you and your close friends.

When someone calls your office number and your agency or practice does not handle emergencies, they will likely hear a common message: if they are having an emergency, they should call the number for emergency services. Hospitals offer certain levels of care and availability to patients who are experiencing emergencies that you or your agency may not be equipped to handle. For example, most hospitals are open twenty-four hours a day, seven days a week. When you are asleep, hospital staff are working to take care of any crises that happen in the night. Just as your clients should have a number to call in an emergency situation, so should you. So, in a moment of exhaustion and weariness that is far more clinical, please have at the ready emergency numbers you can call, including but not limited to numbers for suicide prevention hotlines.

Questions

1. Do you remember why you wanted to be a mental health professional? If so, what was the reason?

2. What do you usually think about when feeling exhausted? If your thoughts are mostly negative and draining, how can you work on changing your pattern of what you reflect on after reading this chapter?

3. If you have never made a list or journaled an amazing adventure you had with God, is it possible to look back at chapter two on the characteristics of God and reflect on one of God's traits? If so, which characteristic would you focus on?

5: Be Still and Study

Have you ever tried to take a test without studying? I confess I have more times than I care to count or freely admit at this time. The majority of the time it worked out well because I was able to retain enough from sitting through lectures. However, at times I hoped for a testing miracle. When I was in school, I prayed the hardest during test time. Tests were much easier to take after I took time to reread the chapters and my notes. I was not just guessing at answers, hoping I remembered right; I had confidence I was choosing the correct answers.

Did you sit for your licensing examination right after finishing your degree? Some people with exceptional memories of all their course materials might have, but the rest of us had to have a study plan and study materials. You may have read books, listened to audio lessons in your car, and used flashcards to remember all the theories and interventions along with many other professional details you needed to be able to recall during examination time. Whatever your study method, you were prepared when it was time to be tested.

Now, I have a test for you. You are talking to a loved one on the phone. This could be a family member or a friend.

For some reason your conversation changes from kind to slightly hostile. The other person starts yelling at you, and before you can say anything else hangs up the phone. What do you do next?

A. Call the person back, saying equally mean things, and then hang up the phone on them.
B. Drive to their house and yell back at them.
C. Send an angry text message in a group text of other people who angered you that day.
D. Wait until you both are calm and call to rationally talk through what happened.

If you choose A, B, or C, your answer would be biblically incorrect. If you have ever chosen one of these in a real-life scenario, then you know they would likely escalate the conflict. Depending on your relationship to that person, doing or saying something that you may later regret may not have been worth losing or damaging that relationship. Sometimes, depending on what has happened in such a situation, it is very tempting to respond with one of those first three answers.

However, if you had studied for this test, you would have found the answer in many verses in the Bible that could have served as a guide on what to do when you feel angry with someone. Here is an example: "A hot-tempered person stirs up conflict, but one slow to anger calms strife" (Proverbs 15:18). So, based on this verse the answer to the above question would be D. Life can be a continual stream of tests similar to this one, and if you have the right answers planted firmly in your memory and heart, though you will not live perfectly, you will be better prepared to respond to life the way God prefers.

Making God's Word Personal

Do you have someone in your life you can call when you need to talk, someone who seems to have memorized the Bible because they have a biblical answer to any subject you bring up? Are you that friend? Do you want to be that friend? How about being that friend to yourself? If you want to be able to hold God's Word so close to your heart that you go through your day in meditation on His Word and what it means in your life, then you will do what we did in school—study.

Studying the Bible may look different for each of us, and I encourage you to find your own way. Pray before you figure out your way, asking God to help you understand His Word and keep it firm in your heart and mind. If you need a specific method, there are many resources available on how to study the Bible. If you did not want to study alone or feel that you do not have the self-discipline to continue to study past one day, you may need the structure and accountability of a Bible study group at your church. If you have the kind of work schedule that could conflict with the times most Bible studies are offered, consider studying with a friend or colleague during your lunch. If you are shaking your head right now because none of these options work for you, then look for Bible studies available online. Whatever plan you come up with, I pray God blesses your study time.

The Bible has been translated into many languages and many times over in English. Personally, I have more than one Bible (because honestly with some verses I understand one translation better than another) and a Bible app on my phone. It is also a click away on my computer, and when I am driving, I can listen to it through my car speakers. There are so many ways that you can study the Bible, and because of the continuing advancement in technology, it seems that the Bible is available in English in almost any learning modality. Because of the progress in translation of the Bible into various languages, the same could probably easily be said for other languages.

Think about studying for your licensure or certificate examination again. When you were studying one of the counseling theories on development, you could have chosen to remember the stages in two ways. You could have looked at the names of stages and nothing else, or you could have thought of someone you know or have known at each stage. The second way would have made it more meaningful, and you may have remembered the information better because you made it personal, thinking about it longer than just looking at the words. With the Bible right at our fingertips, it can be tempting to get that Bible-verse-of-the-day text, forward it to a few people, and feel as though we have done our Bible studying for the day. But think about it—have we studied that verse in a meaningful way? Have we considered what it means for any length of time and how to apply it to our own lives?

Here's an example: "Jesus wept" (John 11:35 - ESV). This may be one of the first verses children learn if they grow up in a Christian, Bible-reading household. It is easy to remember because it is short. As you grow older and your vocabulary expands, you understand it says Jesus cried, and when someone is weeping it is much more than just a gentle roll of a tear down the cheek. Once you read the verse in context to know what actually occurred, you see that Jesus had just asked about the dead body of a dear friend whom He was about to raise from the dead. After Jesus was invited to follow the individuals to go and see the body, He began weeping (John 11:34-35 - ESV). This gives you a whole different understanding of what may have seemed to you as a child as just a simple verse.

When I was a child, I spent many summers in vacation Bible school and many Sundays in Sunday school. If you had this experience too, you may remember at some point having to memorize Bible verses. Some of these same Bible verses are still the truths of God that hold me during all the seasons and circumstances of life. For example, as I mentioned in the chapter on prayer, I often find myself waiting in long lines at the store. Sometimes I think I somehow purposely choose the longest line. During some of these times, I repeat the following in my head: "Love is patient." This is the beginning of verse 4 of the 1 Corinthians 13 verses that discuss the characteristics of love. If you want to read or memorize the rest of the verses, they can be found in 1 Corinthians 13. In that same letter to the Corinthians, Paul wrote, "Let all that you do be done in love" (16:14 - ESV).

If love is patient, among other things, and we are to do everything in love, then I must wait patiently because that is how to lovingly wait in a very long line. After reflecting on how these verses apply to my circumstances, I am at the register and almost out of the door. See how meditating on God's Word can apply even in what may seem like the smallest of circumstances?

Memorizing God's Word

If studying and memorizing God's Word can get me through a checkout line, then I am confident it can get someone through a rough day or a period of time when they need to learn to practice self-care from a spiritual point of view. When your soul needs a good meal, why not feed it the Word of God? When you are hungry, you do not go to the grocery store where the food is, look around, then leave. Instead, you buy some food items and take them home to cook a meal or make a snack. When you are done cooking, you do not make a plate and just stare at the food, smelling it and hoping to get full. You will not get the full extent of the satisfaction and nutrients the food provides until the food is in your stomach. Your body needs nutrients.

With the food in your stomach, your hunger is gone. Depending on what you have eaten, you know you have done a good thing for your body. Your soul and God's Word can be the same way. It would not be enough for you to just go to a Christian bookstore and look at the Bibles or to buy one and bring it home, set it on your coffee table or bedside table, and never read it. To fully digest the Word of God, you have to read it and think about what it means personally. If you want to go a step further, you could write a meaningful verse on a note card or, if it works better for you, type it into a note on your phone, then walk around with your verse all week to memorize it. Then when you have one of those moments when you need to remember how God intended for us to love one another, you will have committed a verse to memory.

If memorizing one verse a week is too much of a challenge at first, then be flexible and honest with yourself about what you are willing to do. What do you do when your clients do not complete their homework assignments? You both figure out how to make the goal more realistic and easier to attain. You can do the same thing for yourself. Maybe you will have a verse a month or a few verses to take you through this time in life—or one verse the whole year. But if you think about it, even if it took you one year to memorize a Bible verse, that would be one more verse than you knew the year before.

Studying and memorizing God's Word provides peace for your spiritual health, which is as important as taking care of yourself physically and emotionally. If you can hold on to God's Word during a season of weariness or struggle, you can hold on to God's promises for your life, and the hope that comes with knowing God's love, power, and strength can sustain you. Because this book is about self-care during difficult times, I have highlighted how God's Word can uphold you when life is tough; however, holding God's

Word close to your heart is good all the time—when life is going great for you, when you feel as though God has blessed you in so many ways you could not possibly ask or expect anything more, and when life is unremarkable, when everything is fine.

Starting Your Studying

Of the many ways to engage God's Word, I have found my studying most meaningful when I can think of how the verse or verses apply personally. But if you are just beginning to learn about the Bible, then you may not know how to start. Should you read it from cover to cover, start with the New Testament, start with the Proverbs, or read it in chronological order? There are many options for you to choose from as you are beginning. Other options are devotional books created for certain seasons of life and daily readings on certain topics.

If you want to search for something specific in the Bible and you are unsure of where to even begin to find it, you have two choices. First, if this is your first time to actually read the Bible, I encourage you to start with one that has a topical index in the back. Most Bibles have one. Are you having difficulty being forgiving? Flip to the index and then find all the Scriptures that refer to forgiveness.

If perhaps you have a Bible without an index or you are using an online Bible, then a quick search will provide you with the information you are seeking. When searching online for anything related to God's Word, look for an honest and reliable source. Many websites simply have the opinions of other people, and some of it may not be supported by actual facts. This is the same for some websites that seek to explain biblical principles. One good way to know you may need to think twice about what you are reading is if the material does not include any Scriptures to validate its points, or the verses are being taken out of context. You will know whether a verse is being used in context by looking at the verse and then reading a few lines above and below the verse you are studying. Once you find a reputable information source, then you can choose to use it while you continue to learn the answers to the questions you may have.

The second way you can start your studying as a new student of God's Word is to join a group study. If you live in an area with many churches, you might have a variety of different group studies to choose from. Some churches meet in a large group format similar to a church service. Other churches have more of a classroom setup with small group meetings, and some of these include in-depth discussion. If you are unable to meet in a group setting but still feel that you need accountability, or you know that you will begin studying alone but not follow through with your plan, then having at least one other study partner may be beneficial. Reading through a book of the Bible or a biblical topic with others can be helpful because your fellow group members can help you answer your questions as you work better at understanding for yourself, which takes us to the next section.

Reading and Understanding for Yourself

Have you ever been to a country where the people did not speak your language, and you had to rely on an interpreter to communicate with everyone around you? You likely trusted your interpreter to communicate correctly what you said and what others said to you. However, you would have no lingering doubt if you spoke the language yourself and could speak freely with those around you. If you know the correct words yourself, then your comfort level with communication increases and your confidence in your comprehension grows.

I often hear or read statements that people think are quoted directly from God's Word, but they are not. They may be paraphrased, but they are not exact, and oftentimes they may be used to justify an individual's behavior without taking any other verses on the topic into consideration. When you are writing a research paper, you do not just take one journal article and start writing from that one. Instead, you would choose a few different ones on your topic and combine what you have learned to gain a greater perspective.

For example, have you ever heard "spare the rod, spoil the child" spoken as if it were a Bible verse? That exact statement is not there, yet some people attempt to use this "verse" to guide their discipline techniques for their children. The verse that is close to the saying can be found in Proverbs 13:24: "The one who will not use the rod hates his son, but the one who loves him disciplines him diligently." I am not going to enter my opinion here on whether or not parents should use corporal punishment to correct their children, but I do want to call your attention to the real instruction in the Bible from which the saying is based. If you are a clinician working with children, you know the importance of limit setting and age-appropriate consequences to increase a child's likelihood of having a future as a self-disciplined adult. However, just saying, "spare the rod, spoil the child," without an in-depth study of what the proverb that is being paraphrased really means, can lead to, in the worst-case scenario, an unhealthy application of the verse.

When you think about this using the research paper example, you will find that if you were looking for biblical understanding on how to raise children, other verses would also be helpful, including Proverbs 22:6 and Ephesians 6:4. If you read these verses, you would learn that children should be taught correctly from the time they are small (the Proverbs verse) and in the ways of the Lord not being incited to anger (the Ephesians verse). See, the more you study, the more you will find.

People say other things that are loose interpretations of the verses themselves or complete misinterpretations. For example, have you ever heard someone say they would treat people like people treat them because that is the Golden Rule? The verse they are referring to is Matthew 7:12: "Therefore, whatever you want others to do for you, do also the same for them, for this is the Law and the Prophets." So, what we are actually called to do here is to treat people the way we would want them to treat us. You would likely not want someone to treat you in a rude manner, and so you should not treat someone else that way, even if they were treating you rudely first. Think about it—if you return the favor by treating them rudely in retaliation, then when will it stop? You can stop the animosity before it gets too far by simply responding in a way that you would want someone to respond to you.

People use other verses, and with a missing word or two, the wrong meaning of the verse is passed from one generation to the next. For example, you may have heard it said that money is the root of all evil. According to the Bible, it is not the money that is evil, it is the love of it (1 Timothy 6:10). This is more about a condition of the heart than it is about the tangible object. So, if you have money, unless you know something that I do not, it is not likely evil in itself. It does not have evil thoughts, plans, or actions. It just sits there waiting to be spent or saved. However, an individual who loves money, who goes out to do immoral, illegal things to obtain the money that they so admire, would be giving us an application of what the verse really means.

Would you know if someone was giving you wrong or misinterpreted information from the Bible? The only way to know for sure is to know God's Word for yourself. If you do not know God's Word to the point that you have many verses memorized, but you have at least done some studying, you would be more likely to recognize whether or not someone is passing on God's truths to you. Much like a test you have studied for, you will have a certain degree of assurance when you can understand the Scriptures for yourself.

The more I learn about God's Word, the more I stand in awe of this love letter the Father has given to us. Through the Scriptures we learn what God expects from us, how much He loves us, historical facts of what occurred before it was our turn to grace Earth with our presence, and what is to come in the future. I have found that the more biblically knowledgeable I am about something, the less I am surprised, and the more peace I find in the coming of our Lord Jesus. For example, some people may become confused or frustrated at the fact that the world is becoming increasingly immoral and evil appears to be rampant. People are worshipping, applauding, and encouraging what we know to be wrong and mocking those who criticize what we believe to be immoral.

You can take this mockery in two ways. You can become discouraged at what the world has turned into, or you can sit back in awe of God, grateful for His warning that this was going to happen and more grateful to know Jesus is closer to being on His way. Specifically, God's Word states,

> But understand this, that in the last days there will come times of difficulty. For people will be lovers of self, lovers of money, proud, arrogant, abusive, disobedient to their parents, ungrateful, unholy, heartless, unappeasable, slanderous, without self-control, brutal, not loving good, treacherous, reckless, swollen with conceit, lovers of pleasure rather than lovers of God, having the appearance of godliness, but denying its power. Avoid such people (2 Timothy 3:1–5 - ESV).

By knowing these last difficult days include such people and behaviors, we will have less of a shock when we see the world changing, because we have already been warned.

Additionally, if one of the reasons you are feeling the sting of burnout or the heavy heart of weariness is your discouragement over the negative state of humanity, then knowing 2 Timothy 3:1–5 may give you a different perspective. A biblical perspective like this may readjust your expectations of people's behavior and subsequently your feelings about that behavior.

Similar to the discussion of prayer and finding your own time and place to meet with God, only you know your schedule and your learning style, so use that information to make decisions about how to get started and how often to study. You can buy all the index cards you want, but if you know this is not how you prefer to memorize things, then choose your own method. Ask God to guide your Bible study time, and remember that your studying is about providing your soul with spiritual nourishment, not just adding another activity to your list of things to do. The more you study God's Word, the more you will learn about how to be still and rest in Him.

Questions

1. What is your favorite Bible verse? Why?

2. In what way are you meaningfully studying God's Word? If you have not yet, in what way can you begin to study God's Word?

3. What Bible verse(s) have you committed to memory to help you through life stressors?

6: Be Still and Say No

Have you ever been to a self-serve buffet-style restaurant? If not, have you ever been to a buffet where you were separated from the server by glass? If you or the server places too much food on your plate, either some of it will fall off on your way to the table or you will not be able to eat it all in one setting. Only you know how much should go on your plate. Some people have bigger appetites than you and can eat a heavily filled plate and go back for two more, and others may only be able to eat half of one lightly filled plate. Something else to contemplate here is what you might consider a full plate one day may not be a full plate on another day. For example, if this is your favorite restaurant and you have not eaten in two days, then you might eat one full plate, a salad, and a dessert. The next day you may have lunch with a friend, and so at dinner the only thing you are able to eat comfortably is the salad and a dessert.

Know Your Ratio

Only you know how hungry you are for a meal. Only you know how much you want to eat and how much your stomach can hold in that moment. Similarly, only you know how much you can do before sleepiness sets in for the day. Only you know how much you can work or complete any daily activities before you need to stop because you require rest or sleep. Call this your activity/tiredness ratio. When you are at the buffet and full, you do not make another plate just to sit there and look at it or try to eat the food anyway, because your stomach can hold no more. If you try to, you may have great discomfort and some type of gastrointestinal distress. So, unless you have a clinical issue working against you, when you have had enough, you stop. We can do this with our eating, yet some people struggle with limiting their activities when it comes to working with or helping other people beyond the point where they have the time and energy. Some enjoy being busy and have a difficult time sitting still, but others just have a hard time telling people no.

Some days you will have more of an appetite for food than other days. Along these lines, some days you will have more energy to do certain activities than other days. One could assert this is the same way life works for everyone, in particular for a helping professional. Some days you may have more emotional and spiritual energy to take on all the tasks ahead of you, everything on your work plate. However, there may be times in your life when your plate is full, and someone asks you to add one more thing to it. You know, based on your previous experiences, if you add one more thing to your plate, something else is going to fall off. One of your tasks will go undone or will be only partially completed. Even worse, you will do them all, knowing it is too much (the equivalent of continuing to eat past the point of fullness), and could set yourself up for exhaustion, fatigue, or absolute burnout.

Earlier I made mention of an activity/tiredness (or daily activity/I am tired now and can do no more) ratio. A better description may be the ratio of busy activity to restful activity, because you really should stop to rest before you get to the point where you have to say to yourself or anyone else, "I am tired and can do no more." Before you get to the point where you can do no more, it is likely that your body and/or mind were already sending you signals that rest is needed.

When you are "on," then you are actively working. You could be on the job, volunteering, cleaning your house, taking care of your family, having fun with your friends or whatever other responsibilities and activities you engage in during your busy week, but you are not technically "off" until you are resting. Have you ever come home from a vacation needing to rest for a day or two before going back to work? It is because during the vacation you were "on." You were following an activity-filled schedule, planning excursions, finding new places to eat, and running to and from the car or airport. Once you were home and too tired to do any more, then you turned "off" to do something more restful, like watch movies or take a nap.

It is important to be honest with yourself and the fact that there are only twenty-four hours in a day. As much as some people would like to, it is probably not the healthiest for you to be constantly on the go for the majority of that time. Many people do not get enough sleep every night, but if you sleep from seven to eight hours, you then have sixteen to seventeen hours of awake time. In that sixteen or seventeen hours, you will need time to sit and rest. You get to choose when and how much time, but if you do not rest, then your busy activity/restful activity ratio will likely not be in a healthy range.

Saying a Loving No

You were in classes learning the theories and skills related to your profession, and you said yes to typing all those papers. You said yes to hours of study time and to going to class when you would have rather been doing something more entertaining. If you have a doctorate degree, you then said yes to a dissertation process and likely without hesitation spent more time than you can remember editing it until you may have had portions of it memorized. When you were a practicum student or an intern, you said yes to your supervisor's directives and tasks in order to complete your hours, time, or other professional requirements. You may have been a yes-person only during your school and training process, or you may be one of those people who just has a difficult time saying no. Some people are just "yes" people, and the idea of saying no causes more discomfort than the fatigue they feel from taking on too many tasks.

If you find you cannot be still due to a lack of enough time each day, you may have overfilled your schedule. In these times, if someone wants to add one more thing to your already busy schedule, then you may find it necessary to say no. If you cringe at the thought of having to tell someone no so you can get some rest, then you may want to examine why you would rather do something you have no time for instead of politely refusing their request.

If studied at some length, I am sure we could find many ways to say no to someone in a manner that honors God. Here we will look at this through the lens of the fruit of the Spirit. "But the fruit of the Spirit is love, joy, peace, patience, kindness, goodness, faithfulness, gentleness, self-control; against such things there is no law" (Galatians 5:22–23 - ESV). Look at a few of the ways you could say no: lovingly, peaceably, patiently, kindly, and gently. In a society where people encourage one another to be rude, blunt, and petty, it has become increasingly important to remember to say things in a loving manner, including the word *no*.

Oftentimes, people have a hard time saying no to something that may not be in their best interest because they can find plenty of reasons to say yes. One of your reasons may be that when you do whatever it is yourself, you will have confidence that it is done the way you prefer. However, if you are so tired from everything you do, consider how much better you could perform when you were well-rested. These new tasks, when it is not absolutely necessary that you are the one responsible for them, could be left to others who are quite capable of doing them.

When someone else is able to complete the task you are being asked to do, then it is time to say no in a loving way. One of the first things you want to note is that for the sake of your relationship with the individual who is asking you, it is important to say no in a kind manner. You may even thank the individual for thinking of you before letting them know kindly that you are unable to do what they are asking for. Be mindful of your vocal tone. Look back at the fruit of the Spirit list. When you say no, are you speaking gently? Some people have naturally gentle voices and whatever they say sounds kind, and you just hope that they would be the person on your outgoing message to your voicemail because their voices are so soothing. But there are others who do not naturally have a gentle tone of voice, and thus even if they are saying something nice, the message sounds harsh. If your voice is the latter, then you may need to practice your gentle *no* with someone who loves you dearly and is willing to honestly help you find your gentle but genuine vocal tone. Choose an honest friend. The one you can ask, "Did that sound gentle enough?," and if it does not, then they can lovingly, kindly, and gently tell you "no."

When we were in school, we learned about nonverbal behavior and how to spot and point out the discrepancies when therapeutically necessary. In this same way, it may be good to do an honest self-check. Your voice may be saying you're trying to turn down the offer to do an activity in a nice way, but your body language and facial expressions may be giving an entirely different message. It is possible that if you are feeling agitated about what you are being asked to do and are not mindful of nonverbal communication, this may come across to the individual requesting for you to do something. Watch for this, maybe practicing in a mirror or with someone, all the while remembering, "Let all that you do be done in love" (1 Corinthians 16:14 - ESV).

Learning to Say No

Another reason you may say yes at a time when you probably should not is you may be putting the needs of the person who asked you for something ahead of your own. A person who can put the needs of others ahead of their own has a heart of gold, and I am in no way discouraging this behavior. As children of God it is important that we are in a place to take care of each other. Specifically, we can look to the Bible for instruction: "Do nothing out of selfish ambition or conceit, but in humility consider others as more important than yourselves. Everyone should look out not only for his own interests, but also for the interests of others" (Philippians 2:3-4). When you are feeling the pangs of burnout, saying no to one or two activities that can be done by someone else may be in the best interest of your emotional and spiritual well-being. Once you are refreshed, then there is no reason you cannot go back to being the selfless person you are naturally, or that you are growing to be spiritually.

One way to be sure you are saying yes to only what you are absolutely capable of doing with your full self is to pray about what you are being asked before giving an answer. If you have a full plate already and you have been asked to do one more thing, are you convinced God is sending this task to you, or are you saying yes because...

1. you assume if you say no, no one else will complete the task;
2. you are so accustomed to saying yes to that person that you are afraid to hurt their feelings by saying no; or
3. you went into this profession as a helper of people and find it too uncomfortable to say no to helping anyone who asks?

Doing some of your own research will reveal a list of ways to say no, but I will not provide a list here because in my humble opinion, your no should be from your heart and in your own words. Often, the difficult part is waiting patiently for God's answer to your prayers on whether you should proceed. Sometimes we barge ahead. When God's answer is yes, there would be no need to say no; when God's answer is no, let yours also be a loving and kind no.

After reading this, some people will continue to have a difficult time saying no. One of the reasons to say no to some things is the energy required to stay alert in assisting your clients, actively listening to them, and using all of the other intervention techniques you have learned. As hard as it is to say no, it would be more difficult to listen as actively and attentively as your clients need you to when you are exhausted. So, if you have had a difficult time in the past saying no when you are already at your capacity for activity, consider saying no for the sake of being more well-rested for the things you have already committed to. Remember, you have only so much time in your day, and when you begin to incorporate some time for being still, you have less for other things.

Learning to Delegate

As a mental health professional, some duties are solely yours. You are the clinician for your clients, so your duty is to provide clinical services and to write case notes and psychological reports. However, you can delegate some duties in your life to others whenever it is possible, either professional or personal, such as making copies or running errands. For example, when you are at work, you could make all the copies you need, or you could have someone assist you while you take care of something else, such as using that one or two minutes just to sit still. When you get home, you could run all your own errands, but if you have someone who is willing to help you, you could allow them to do that, taking the errands off of your plate.

Sometimes people are unwilling to delegate because they feel they would lose control. Others believe anyone helping them will be unable to do it in the same manner or at the same quality level as they would. If this latter individual is you, then this is a good time to learn to be a good teacher. If you prefer to have the paper in the breakroom arranged in a certain way, teach an assistant how to do it. If you live with a family in your house and you like the living room to be cleaned in a certain way, teach someone who is not as busy as you to arrange pillows and vacuum the way you prefer. These may not be any of the issues you are dealing with, so think about other tasks you can give to the willing helpers around you. Have you never delegated that task before? Consider whether it is something you might be able to do.

When you have decided that you are able to delegate more of the tasks that you do not necessarily have to do yourself, and while teaching someone else the task, you still feel that you can do a better job, pray for patience. It is possible that because it is a task you have been doing for many years, it seems very simple to you. However, someone who has no idea of what to do will need more time to learn. Remember when someone had to be patient with you, and if you cannot recall a time, God is patient with us every day. Remember that even if teaching them is taking more of your time now, eventually if taught and learned correctly, it should free up your time later, and that is the end goal—to give you more time to rest. So, in this way you are lovingly telling yourself no to having more tasks on your plate than is necessary.

Saying No to Persuasives

One of the hardest parts of saying no in love is saying it to that individual who is accustomed to getting their way through very persuasive means. Some people have a most difficult time with accepting and understanding that you do not want to do something or cannot possibly do anything else with your already filled schedule. With this person, you may have to say no repeatedly in the same setting. Remember, what others may deem selfish will be your healing from your weariness, and by doing so, you are doing the best thing for your clients, patients, and/or students.

For the sake of your weary soul, avoid falling into the persuasive's trap by allowing them to tell you how much more you can handle. You are only one person with only so much time in the day; a little assertiveness will go a long way. Some persuasives, once you give them a reason for not doing something, will provide a fix for that reason to simply get you to do what they want you to do. The conversation may go something like this.

Persuasive: "Hey, can you help me with this project? I have to have it done by tomorrow at 1:00 p.m."

So this individual needs something done by the next day. Between the time they ask you and their deadline, you have clients to see, your only break being your lunchtime. You have read the chapter in this book "Be Still and Pray" and decided you will have a moment of quiet time with God while you eat lunch away from the office for the first time in years. You have made this decision because you are feeling weary and are trying to take better care of yourself, so you respond:

You: "I'm sorry, but I don't have the time to help you."

Look at that—a nice, kind, and gentle no (if you said it with a gentle tone and without folded arms or eye rolling). But then the persuasive responds.

Persuasive: "Could you help me for a while during your lunch breaks today and tomorrow? I really need help, and you are so knowledgeable on the topic of this project."

Unless you work in an emergency room or are required

to handle the emergencies where you work, most people's emergencies are all their own. If you know you are unable to help, even though the persuasive is attempting to reel you in by pointing out how good you are at something, you may suggest a competent person who can help in your place who also has more time than you.

You: "I know it is very important for you to get this done, but I have made plans for lunch and prayer over the next couple of days. Perhaps _____ can help you?"

Persuasive: "You know, I can bring you lunch for the next two days, and we can work together while you eat."

I am going to stop the back and forth here because I just wanted to give you a small illustration, but you should know the persuasive usually does not give up easily. If you persist on going out of the office for lunch, this individual may ask to go to lunch and pray with you because they also have things to pray about. If this happens, you have two choices. You can take the time alone, following the Lord's example when He went to pray in secluded places, and you can stand firm in your decision to say no with love. Or you can invite them to pray and eat lunch with you, and when work comes up, simply redirect the conversation back to prayer and lunch.

In this latter situation, as soon as you begin to eat or pray, they may start asking questions about the help they need for work. Remember this the next time this individual asks for help. They may not respect your boundaries, as far as needing to be refreshed in the Lord is concerned. Having to redirect the person in conversation may be emotionally draining during a time when you had intended to (and likely needed to) take a break. This is just one example of a persuasive, but be on the lookout for individuals who may try to talk you out of your peace, especially when they encroach on the time slated just for you and the Father.

When you have a yes spirit, learning to say no when it is in your best interest may be one of the hardest things you have to learn to do. If you have ever had to write a thesis or dissertation, it can be harder than that. How can you learn to be still and present (physically, spiritually, and emotionally) in the company of God if you are always too busy? As you begin to appreciate the extra time you can have to be present alone with God, and your loving no becomes a healthy habit when necessary, you may begin to notice something. Some, but not all, of the people who were accustomed to your consistent yes behavior may begin to treat you differently due to however they feel (i.e., disappointed). When you need to refresh your weary soul, their feelings and changed behavior toward you may tempt you to change course because of the way it makes you feel (i.e., guilty). Remember the reason you said no in the first place, and contemplate if the person cares about you or what you do for them.

As you are learning to say no, you may begin to think that you are in some ways being selfish. However, saying no to some things so you can be refreshed as both a therapist and an individual is not solely about you. This is because you eventually will be in contact with another person who is either getting a fatigued version of you or a well-rested version of you. Doing things for yourself when you need to, for your body, mind, and soul, even when it is solely about you feeling better is all right, too. Remember, when your clients have a refreshed mental health practitioner to process their life stressors, they have a better version of you than one who is drained of all of their energy. This is the same for the other people in your life, including your loved ones, your friends, your colleagues and co-workers, and whoever else you can add to your own personal list.

Questions

1. When was the last time you said no to something you had no time for?

2. If you need to say no in the future, how can you do so in a loving manner?

3. What do you think are some of the reasons either you or others have difficulty saying no?

7: Be Still and Take Care

Once many years ago, I went to the grocery store to buy eggs and learned a very important lesson. I got the eggs and put them in the basket, being careful every step of the way once they were in my care. I carefully placed them on the conveyer belt beside the cashier and slowly placed them back in the basket to get them to the car. I put all my other grocery bags in my car first before putting the bag with the eggs on the car seat. The eggs and I made it all the way home without incident. But the next morning it happened. What happened? Good question. I went in the kitchen to make eggs for breakfast and noticed that four of them were cracked. Since I had been careful getting them home, I can only assume they were broken when I purchased them. I should have checked them before I left the store.

The lesson I learned here is that the outside of the egg protects the inside, which is the more useful part of the egg when it will be your breakfast. The inside of the egg will most likely be the more useful part in any situation, unless you are a craft person who has made some eggshell masterpieces, or if you do not eat eggs for some reason. But for this illustration, I will say that the inside of the egg is what makes the egg. Without the yolk and egg white, all you have is the shell. This does not make the shell unimportant. It is quite the opposite. The shell is essential to ensuring the egg's insides can be useful when it is time.

While I set out to write a book about mental healthcare professionals being able to find time to refresh themselves spiritually, I cannot end this discussion without addressing the temple that our souls live in (the outer shell). Yes, we must take care of the temple too, which is how your body is described in the Bible. "Don't you realize that your body is the temple of the Holy Spirit, who lives in you and was given to you by God? You do not belong to yourself" (1 Corinthians 6:19 - NLT). Many of the self-care techniques that we have already learned while studying mental health interventions, such as eating healthy foods, sleeping enough, and having a good social support network, are options for taking care of our outer shell. I will discuss some of what we need to take care of the outer shell only briefly in this chapter, because I do want to keep the focus on spiritual health.

Of course, you should always consult with a physician on lifestyle changes to ensure you are making those changes in a healthy manner. Also, I am not giving you advice on what you should do to keep yourself physically healthy, because that is your physician's job. However, I think it is important to ask yourself whether or not you have healthy habits. When people question their own mental health, they call to consult with you. Likewise, if you are feeling you may not be caring for your physical health as well as you should, you should consider going to see the doctor.

Your Physical Health

When your clients come to see you, they are taking care of their mental health and seeking to feel better or to learn to think of a life situation in a healthy, rational manner. They either are in search of the answer to their symptoms (their diagnosis) or therapeutic intervention (individual or group counseling) for issues they already recognize. On the other hand, there are those who show up to your office who are mandated to be there by some agency or the court or were strongly encouraged by a loved one, and their insight into the issue may be limited or nonexistent. The same situation relates to your body. When was the last time you had a physical, a dental checkup, or any other checkup you may need? Sometimes as helpers, we can get so caught up helping that we neglect to be helped ourselves when we need it, or in the case of a preventative yearly physical, before we need it. Just as there are some people who enter our offices because they were strongly encouraged by a loved one or friend, you may have those people in your life who have suggested that you schedule a checkup. Are you listening to them? When your own doctor asks you to come back in for a follow-up, are you following your doctor's orders?

We need those other health and helping professionals to help keep our outer shell ready to report for duty every day. If you are not feeling well or you have a bad toothache, how much time do you spend listening to your clients, and how much time do you spend wishing that you were in bed healing, sipping soup broth, and watching television? Even if it is for a valid reason, a distracted mind is a distracted mind. In the case of a painful experience related to your teeth, working in coordination with your dentist may give you the opportunity to get the problem taken care of before you are crying in pain or distracted by it while you are meeting with a client.

Your Eating Habits

Taking care of your physical health includes your eating habits. I know I have given many food examples throughout the book, because food is important. The nutrients you put into your body fuel you for the rest of the day. Most people will stop and willingly take a lunch break at a job that they do not enjoy. They may have their watches or mental clocks set to the time to take that lunch, eager to get out of the building or at least to stop their work for a while. However, when your job is exciting to you and something that you cannot wait to do every day, then you do not mind incorporating your lunch into work, making it a working lunch. But should you?

I know some of our schedules make it difficult to have a real lunch, which can result in not eating at all or having a working lunch that may not be exactly nourishing. You may just be looking for something to eat to stop your stomach from growling, so you eat some old crackers you found in your desk and some candy you found on another person's desk. Be honest with yourself about what your body needs and take some time to properly fuel yourself. If you have or suspect that you may need to have special dietary restrictions, please be sure to speak with your doctor or the professional (i.e., nutritionist) you consult about proper nutrition to ensure you are getting your daily dose of what your body needs. While it might be tempting to follow a dietary fad or the newest diet for weight loss or weight gain, not having the appropriate nutrients for your specific body needs may be unhealthy.

Your Sleep

Have you ever read the story in the Bible about Jesus calming the storm that surrounded the boat He and His disciples were in (Mark 4:35–41)? If you have never heard of the story, Jesus and His disciples were in a boat when a storm struck suddenly and began to fill their boat with water. As the water filled the boat, the disciples found Jesus asleep and woke Him with cries about whether He cared that they may die. Jesus calmed the storm and then asked the disciples why they were afraid at all.

I have thought through this scene several times. Every time, depending on what is going on in my life, I learn a different lesson. Out of all the lessons and interpretations I have processed, one is the possibility of sleeping through a storm. While the storm was raging, Jesus was sleeping. Have you ever had a sleepless night because of your own storm? If you have, you are not alone. The next time you are tempted to stay up all night trying to decide what to do in the storm around you, consider the importance of sleep. Jesus walked this earth fully man but also fully God, and let's face it, He could have warned the waves to behave before He went to sleep. Because He did not, the disciples learned important lessons that night, including having faith in God even when you think the storm is going to drown you. From your human perspective, the winds, the waves, and the water filling your boat may be too much, but all of those things are not too big for God. The next time you are having a sleepless night and trying desperately to get your brain to turn off, remind yourself of the power of a God who never sleeps, and be still.

Even though something is possible, that does not mean there is a guarantee that it will happen. In the case of sleep, just because it may be possible to sleep through a storm does not mean you will always be able to sleep through one. Sometimes the storms of life can prevent us from having quality, restorative sleep. Sometimes the fear of the water entering the boat while we sleep stops us from being comfortable enough to fall asleep. Then there are times when the thought of the winds and the rains that are coming with tomorrow's storm wake us and we cannot go back to sleep. There are also those times when from pure exhaustion we do fall asleep, but we only sleep for two or three hours. Although many of us have learned techniques to pass on to our clients as an intervention for insomnia, how often do you personally turn to them when you are unable to sleep? Have you ever added prayer to your list? Have you ever asked God to help you sleep, sharing with Him the burdens that are on your mind, so that you can fall and stay asleep? If your sleeplessness is a case of chronic insomnia as the result of a mental or physical health problem, then remember the importance of contacting the health professionals who are there to help you.

Your Rest

If you have a family member, friend, or passing acquaintance who has some training in how to sing, ask them to explain vocal rest. Some doctors may prescribe vocal rest if using your voice could strain your vocal cords. That means no singing, no talking, not even any whispering. A singer's voice is their instrument. In the helping profession, specifically if you provide therapeutic services, your instrument is you. Your voice. Your thoughts. Your emotions. Your memory of everything your client says in that moment and the last few sessions, in order to bring something back up if needed. To an untrained eye it may look as though you are just sitting, listening, and occasionally nodding your head, but you know active listening takes practice and a tremendous amount of energy on your part.

Along with vocal rest, if this is ever recommended to you, you may need to rest in a way that will also be refreshing to your thoughts, emotions, and active listening skills. Here is where being physically still may be needed while you rest. As discussed in the chapter about having alone time with God to pray, if you are living in a situation where you are unable to take a break from people to have a few silent moments, this may be tough. But tough things are not impossible things. In a world where people believe they have to always be plugged in, where they willingly invite distraction into their lives, we must be intentional to be able to sit quietly and still for a few moments, to gather our thoughts and emotions before moving on to the next task.

Your Heathy Social Support Network

The people around you have the ability to provide you with the support you need during happy and joyful times and also sad, defeated and exhausted times. It is not enough to have a social support network; putting the word *healthy* in front of *social* is the key. Having a healthy social support network can give you what you need to be able to navigate through the many adventures of life. Surrounding yourself with unsupportive people or those who cannot do what you consider helpful can be toxic and harmful to you. One-sided relationships are like this, where one person regularly takes more than they give. Choose your network wisely, and be as good of a support person to them as you expect them to be for you.

The people closest to you may encourage and nourish the strengths and gifts given to you. But unfortunately, they may also use those strengths and gifts until you are depleted. They also may use you and hurt you (whether intentionally or not) because they are the ones with whom you have been the most vulnerable. You do not have to stop being vulnerable in healthy relationships, but it is worth taking a second look to determine if you are involved in any toxic relationships. Check to see how those toxic relationships are weighing heavy on your soul, and pray to God for direction on what to do next.

In these days the term "friend" is loosely used and for many reasons, including the ability to literally have a "friend" a click away on a computer or phone application. These can be people you actually know outside of the internet (i.e., family, co-workers, old friends), people you will never meet in person, or people you will eventually get to know more and meet later. Either way, with the invention of social media platforms, the quantity of friendships somehow replaced the quality of friendships. When you are looking to fuel your depleted and weary soul, I feel very comfortable advocating for healthy, quality relationships with a few others over numerous, shallow "friendships." Being surrounded by a healthy social support network provides you with individuals to cheer you on when you are having life successes, someone to comfort you during the trials of life, and an opportunity to have people in your life who are as blessed to have you as you are blessed to have them.

You may be asking yourself, what do the people in your life have to do with your own outer shell? Good question. The short answer, as you may know already, is that being in unhealthy relationships may be stressful, no matter the nature of the relationship. This stress is not necessarily beneficial to the outer shell because of the health problems, complications, and symptoms that may arise and be linked to the stress. So, in this case, be mindful of the people that you allow to come into and stay in your life.

Be Still

Combining everything that has been discussed so far, remember these acts of inviting spiritual rest into your life. Whether or not you have ever thought about it in this way, you have a very important calling, serving those who are mentally and emotionally in need. Additionally, given the human condition and the state of spiritual warfare, brokenhearted people will make appointments with you to discuss psychiatric symptoms, trauma, and/or some type of deep emotional pain. Having to work with people through these issues on a daily basis, it is important for us to remember to take good care of ourselves for our growth and the good of everyone around us. This does not mean you won't ever have a sense of deep exhaustion or emotional distress at some point, no matter how hard you try to avoid it.

In a moment or season of weariness or distress, you have to intentionally pause and remember that God is all-powerful and can fix your situation. You will want to remember that God loves you and how much He loves you, and if you need a reminder, John 3:16 is a good one. In a moment of confusion about a life situation, you have to intentionally focus on the fact that God knows all and will reveal to you what you need to know using His perfect timing. If you are struggling to have an active prayer life and a quiet time with God, then you will have to guard your time to do so deliberately. It will also be good to know how to reflect on positive thoughts, study God's Word, lovingly tell people no, and take care of yourself. Just as you take care of your physical and emotional health, it is also important to take care of your spiritual health. As we make steps to grow closer to God by learning more about Him, praying to Him, and studying His Word, we take steps to care for the part of us people often neglect. If you are weary in all of what you do, God knows. He cares. Be still for a moment, and allow God to soothe your soul with His strength and love as you work to decrease your burnout and increase your desire for the career you have chosen—the one that for many of us is a calling by the Lord. Be strong. Be loved. Be still.

Questions

1. When was the last time you made an appointment with your physician for a yearly physical?

2. What types of activities do you engage in that you would consider self-care for your physical health?

3. The next time you are unable to sleep during a time of stress or when feeling weary, what can you do differently to promote a return to restorative sleep?

Be Still and Read the Good News

If you are wondering how you can have the type of relationship with God where you can be still in Him, His promises, and His Word, let me introduce you to my friend Jesus. If you begin reading the Bible in Genesis, you will learn God created man and woman (Adam and Eve), and in the paradise God created, they had the ability to speak directly with God. Then sin entered the picture, putting a huge strain on the relationship between God and His human creation. The bad news is that (as I wrote earlier) we are all sinners. The Good News is Jesus entered the world as a perfect baby who grew into a perfect man, wholly man and wholly (as well as holy) God. He died on a cross for our sins, as He had none of His own. They put His body in a tomb, and on the third day God the Father raised Him from the dead. The Father loved us so much that He gave His Son as a sacrifice for our sins, so those who believe in Jesus will be saved.

Being saved, or salvation, is the way to be connected to God in a relationship with Him, and the way to that salvation comes only through Jesus. All you have to do is acknowledge you are a sinner and believe that Jesus's sacrifice covers your sins. Very specifically, Romans 10:9

states, "If you confess with your mouth, "Jesus is Lord," and believe in your heart that God raised him from the dead, you will be saved." With your confession and belief, you are saved and have accepted God's gracious gift of eternal life. This is explained in John 3:16, "For God so loved the world, that he gave his only Son, that whoever believes in him should not perish but have eternal life" (ESV).

Earlier, in the "Be Still and Study" chapter, there was a discussion comparing licensure and certificate examination study methods to meditating on God's Word. To truly get an in-depth understanding of repentance and salvation, study the gospel of John. Enjoy your reading, and for some, your newfound knowledge of Jesus.

A Final Word

Well, you officially finished the book—or, wondering what was written on the last page, you skipped to the end before reading the rest. Either way, here you are. Know my prayer for you is that you learn how much God loves you and that you practice self-care for your soul in the place where He put you to serve others. If you are already working in the field, then you know that self-care is something you have to intentionally and purposefully do until it becomes a habit. I'll leave you with this one last question with no answer from me, since it is a personal question for you. If you have not been taking care of your spiritual health, but you want to, what will you do differently tomorrow?

About the Author

Dr. LaRonda Starling is a Licensed Clinical Psychologist and a Licensed Professional Counselor in Texas, a National Certified Counselor, and an adjunct professor at a Christian university. She has earned a Bachelor of Arts degree in Psychology, Master of Science degree in Counseling, and a Doctor of Philosophy degree in Psychology with a specialization in Clinical Psychology. As a clinician, Dr. Starling provides therapeutic services (psychological assessment and counseling) in a private practice setting. Along with her clinical experience as a mental health professional, Dr. Starling has over fifteen years of experience working in academic environments; first as a staff member and then as adjunct faculty in both classroom and online settings. In all that she does (working or volunteering), she hopes that God receives the glory as she uses the gifts He has so graciously given her. Although Dr. Starling has always enjoyed writing, *Be Still: Spiritual Self-Care for Mental Health Professionals* is her first published book.

Grace Psychological
HEALTH SERVICES, PLLC

Website - www.gracepsychserve.com
Instagram - www.instagram.com/gracepsychealth